Absolute Crime Presents:

# Pushed Too Far

*15 Bullying Cases You Will Not Easily Forget*

# ABSO UTE CR ME

By William Webb

**Absolute Crime Books**

**www.absolutecrime.com**

# Table of Contents

# About Us

Absolute Crime publishes only the best true crime literature. Our focus is on the crimes that you've probably never heard of, but you are fascinated to read more about. With each engaging and gripping story, we try to let readers relive moments in history that some people have tried to forget.

Remember, our books are not meant for the faint at heart. We don't hold back — if a crime is bloody, we let the words splatter across the page so you can experience the crime in the most horrifying way!

If you enjoy this book, please visit our homepage to see other books we offer; if you have any feedback, we'd love to hear from you!

# Introduction

Bullying has been viewed as normal for much too long. For too many years, schools, parents and even children and teenagers turned a blind eye to bullying. Because of this attitude, bullies have been allowed to have it their way without receiving any kind of punishment. These stories will show how diverse bullying can be and what tragic consequences it can have. Furthermore, they may suggest solutions to this problem, and may provide inspiration and optimism about the possibility of winning over the bullies.

# Megan Meier

Recently, bullying and cyberbullying have come to the attention of the public as serious issues that need to be stopped. When Megan Meier's story came out in 2006, many could not believe it, and it forced people to recognize cyberbullying as a problem.

Megan Meier was born in 1992 to Christina and Ronald Meier. She grew up near the Dardenne Prairie. As a child, she had self-esteem issues related to her weight. She started visiting a psychiatrist, and was diagnosed with depression and attention deficit disorder. The psychiatrist prescribed citalopram, methyphenidate and ziprasidone.

Up until the 8th grade, Megan attended various public schools, but because of her self-esteem issues, her parents thought she would feel more comfortable in a school with a required a uniform and a no-makeup policy, so they enrolled her at the Immaculate Conception Catholic School in Dardenne Prairie.

Soon after changing schools, Megan opened a MySpace account. She received a message from a boy named Josh Evans. The two of them started to chat on a regular basis on the website, but they never met in real life. For her parents, this new friend seemed like a good thing. They noticed Megan was feeling better and that her mood was completely uplifted by her interactions with Josh.

Josh told Megan that he lived in the nearby town of O'Fallon. He also told her he was homeschooled and that he did not have a phone number. Soon after their "acquaintance" Megan developed a crush on Josh and they started to chat more and more.

On October 16th, the tone in Josh's messages started to change drastically. He told her that he wouldn't want to be friends with her and that she was an awful person to her friends. More messages of this kind were sent, until Josh sent the last message on MySpace, stating again that Megan was a horrible person and that he wished her to have a bad life. The last sentence suggested to Megan that her life was worth nothing and the world would be much better off without her in it. Megan responded to his message, saying she believed him to be a boy that girls would commit suicide over.

20 minutes later, Megan was found hanged by her belt in her closet. She died the very next day, after several failed attempts at resuscitation.

Investigations showed that Josh was not who "he" appeared to be. Lori Drew, the mother of a girl living four doors apart from the Meiers, admitted that she and a few other people, such as her 18-year-old employee, Ashlee Grills, had run the hoax account. As Lori admitted, the account had been opened to torment young Megan because she had allegedly spread rumors about her daughter. According to Lori Drew, the account had started as a joke, but its main purpose was to gain Megan's trust and find out what she truly believed about her daughter (as well as about other people). Later on, investigation showed that the one who had been sending most of the messages to Megan (including the final one that was meant to end the hoax and terminate communication) was Ashlee Grills. However, this was only presented at a press conference in December by Jack Banas, the prosecuting attorney who mentioned that he had not interviewed Ashlee before because she had been under psychiatric treatment. For the most part of the early news reports on the matter, Lori Drew's name remained undisclosed.

It was only one year after Megan's death that her parents started to speak publicly about their story and about all the things that had been revealed during the investigation. When Megan's aunt saw an article about Internet harassment, they contacted the journal and finally talked openly about what had happened. Up to that moment, the FBI asked them to refrain from any kind of public speaking about the matter, as they were still investigating the issue.

Lori Drew was convicted for the violation of the Computer Fraud and Abuse Act in 2008, but her sentence was reversed on appeal a year later. She also reportedly closed the business she had been running (an advertising agency focusing on coupon books) because her name was made public.

When the Suburban Journals published Megan Meier's story, people felt outraged that the Drews' names had still been undisclosed. However, bloggers posted their names, addresses, phone numbers, and a picture of Lori Drew. This led to violations of privacy, vandalism and even Internet stalking. Bandas, the prosecutor who had been investigating Megan's death came out and told everybody that although the Drews cannot be prosecuted, this should not turn into a violation of the law itself.

The reactions stirred by Megan's death and her story were mostly rooted in the idea that an adult could be involved in such an act. In November 2007, a vigil was held for Megan and the event's location was close to the house of the Drew family.

Although the Meier case was not completely resolved and the ones who caused Megan's death were not punished, the case stirred the interest of the authorities. The Board of Aldermen for the city of Dardenne Prairie passed an ordinance in November 2007 prohibiting any kind of harassment over electronic media (including the Internet, text messaging, pagers, etc.), although this harassment is treated as a misdemeanor and is only punished with a fine that goes up to $500 and with up to 90 days of imprisonment. The city of Florissant, Missouri and other cities and states have started to take into account this case and passed similar laws.

Furthermore, Missouri decided to change the laws for harassment because electronic harassment was slipping through the cracks. This is now punished as a felony with up four years of imprisonment if an adult harasses a child under 17 or if the harasser has been previously convicted for harassment.

Missouri was one of the first states to pass a law against cyberbullying and cyber-stalking, but other states have followed suit. The case of Megan Meier raised awareness over the fact that the Internet had become a new medium in which bullies can stalk and harass their victims and that something has to be done in order to protect the children out there from this kind of things happening.

Megan's death is one of the most tragic cases of bullying out there and laws such as those passed by Missouri are meant to prevent this kind of event. For the bubbly and friendly Megan, these laws came too late, but for many other children like her they are one step ahead for their own safety.

It is of the utmost importance that we all acknowledge the fact that bullying is not a way to make kids grow up and that it should be completely intolerable. Many times, both parents and teachers close their eyes when they hear their kids and students are being bullied, because they know that this has been happening for a long time and that they themselves may have been victims of bullying when they were their children's age. Bullying should not be considered the norm and solving this issue starts with acknowledging that, in the end, it is everybody's responsibility to encourage children to be tolerant with each other, instead of being hateful and harmful.

When parents are encouraging bullying, the situation gets completely out of control. In the case of Megan, her death and the fact that the one who came up with the idea was a mother herself shows that there is something wrong with our society – something that needs immediate change.

# Ryan Halligan

As with Megan Meier, Ryan Halligan's story shook the news and raised awareness over the fact that cyberbullying had become a problem and should be punished accordingly. John Halligan, Ryan's father, has been lobbying for the passage of laws to protect children like his son from bullying and to raise awareness in schools about bullying and suicide.

Born in 1989, Ryan had some issues with delayed speech and physical coordination while in his first years of school, but he overcame these issues. As his father recounts, although Ryan was learning much better than he had used to, he still struggled with it. However, the boy never gave up and he always went to school full of optimism.

In 2000, Ryan became a victim of bullying because of his learning issues and because he had a strong passion for music and drama. As his father remembers, kids at school started to bully him and although he tried to get counseling, this was not successful. After moving to a new school, the bullying continued on and off for another two years.

In 2002, Ryan asked his father to buy him a Tae Bo Kick Box set for Christmas because he wanted to learn how to defend himself. Although John wanted to talk to the principal, Ryan believed that it would only worsen the situation and that the bullies would become more aggressive. As a result, John and Ryan started to train together for 2 hours every day. Ryan's father advised him not to pick a fight at school, but he did say that Ryan should defend himself if he was attacked.

Two months after beginning training, Ryan got into a fight at school with a boy that was bullying him. Several months later, he told his father that he and the former bully had become friends and that they were getting along very well. However, the boy seized the opportunity to embarrass Ryan when he told him about an examination he had to undergo for stomach pains. This is where the rumors about Ryan being gay started, rumors which followed the young boy for a long time.

As his father now knows, Ryan spent the next summer over the Internet, on various instant messaging websites and software applications and the bullying about him being gay continued in the online field as well. At the same time, Ryan developed a friendship with Ashley, a popular girl he liked at school. Although she pretended to be friends with him online, she later told him at school that he was a loser, which affected him to the point where he stated that girls like Ashley made him want to kill himself.

Later on, Ryan's father also discovered some very disturbing conversations with a pen pal Ryan had made friends with after Ashley called him a loser. The two boys discussed death, suicide and various means of ending life in a painless way. Even more, the pen pal was encouraging Ryan to actually take the step because it would make his bullies feel bad about it.

Ryan's parents recall him bringing up the issue of suicide with them as well, when he told them about his bad report card. Ryan and his father had a conversation on this topic, but John told his son he would have missed out on some very important moments in their life as a family if he decided to take this step.

At the beginning of October, Ryan hanged himself while the rest of the people in the household were sleeping. It was his sister who found him in his room later that morning.

In an attempt to understand what happened to his child, John Halligan checked his online messages and soon discovered in terror what had been going on with his son over the past few months. Also, he discovered Ryan's yearbook was torn and scribbled over the names of the people who had been tormenting them.

John Halligan met with all the children involved in Ryan's death. The first one who talked to him was Ashley, the girl who told Ryan that he is a loser after pretending to be his friend. Although John Halligan was in pain, he mentioned to Ashley her doing a bad thing does not mean she is a bad person in general. Furthermore, they have appeared on TV to talk against bullying and Ashley still maintains communication with the Halligan family even after they moved away.

After finding out that another boy had laughed about Ryan's death, John Halligan also went to that boy's home. This boy was the one who started the rumor about Ryan being gay. He told him that he wanted to understand how much pain he had caused his son and the boy soon broke into tears asking for forgiveness. Although John initially wanted to press charges against the boy, he was stopped because there was no criminal law to support these charges. Eventually, he forgave both the boy and Ashley.

The boy who had been chatting with Ryan about suicide was the last one John visited. He went to his parents' house and told them that he would not want his discussion with the boy to generate into a dark event. Although the boy's father did not know about the ideas that his son had been having, his mother knew of them and even had a transcript of the discussions. The meeting did not have any result because the woman asked John to leave the house while the father was reading the transcripts.

John has made a series of rules for his other two daughters regarding their activity on the Internet. They are not allowed to chat with strangers and they are forbidden from sharing any kind of personal information with them. Furthermore, they are not allowed to send pictures to strangers and they have a password that is given to them by their father, so that he can check the messages if something happens to them (such as disappearing).

Also, John Halligan has been lobbying for laws that would prevent this from happening ever again to another kid. He has given many speeches in various states to let people know about the effects cyberbullying can have on children and on how this can be prevented. John Halligan believes that such cases are the result of an entire context in which the bullies play an important role, but in which parents and teachers are involved as well. The fact that people accept bullying as a rite of passage is, in Halligan's opinion, one of the first things that must change in order for these cases to disappear.

Vermont passed the Bullying Prevention Policy Law in 2004, as well as the Suicide Prevention law in 2005. The teachers are guided through how they should be dealing with suicide prevention in schools. Furthermore, Ryan's case raised awareness in other states as well and following Vermont, many of them proposed similar laws of their own.

It is sad that the world needs cases such as Ryan's to see that stable laws have to be enacted in order to protect children from suffering from bullying. Instead of unknowingly allowing teenagers to commit suicide because they cannot take the humiliation any longer, we should try to help them. We should try to help them understand themselves as well as their bullies, why they are doing these things and we should try to protect them from being harmed. These kids are obviously sensitive and bullying does nothing else for them than reinforce feelings that should not be there.

The world should not have to see death before it takes precautionary measures and there should definitely be more awareness about how deadly words can be. Words can hurt to the point where adults can take it no more, not to mention teenagers who are already confused by all the changes they are going through.

# Tyler Clementi

In 2010, the world was hit with the news of another suicide. This time, the victim was 18-year-old Tyler Clementi. His story is related both to bullying and to Tyler's recent decision to come out as gay. This raised awareness over both of the issues at hand.

Tyler Clementi was born in 1991 and he was acknowledged as a very talented violinist who played with the Ridgewood Symphony Orchestra, as well as with the Bergen Youth Orchestra. Right before leaving for college at Rutgers, he came out to his parents as being gay. While his father supported him, Tyler believed that his mother completely refused the idea. Later on, his mother stated that she remained silent as it was difficult for her to acknowledge the information she had received, especially due to her evangelical upbringing that clearly stated that homosexuality was a sin. Also, she mentioned that she had felt betrayed by her son for not confiding in her previously. However, she and Tyler spent the rest of the week together and they spoke often while he was at Rutgers.

Dharun Ravi and Tyler met while they were still high-school students. Before arriving at Rutgers, Ravi wanted to find out more about his future roommate and he searched him online. That is when he discovered that Tyler had been posting on the Just Us Boys website. Ravi referred to this on his Twitter account, stating that he had found out his future roommate was gay. Ravi and Tyler rarely spoke and although they were not exactly friends, Tyler appreciated that Ravi did not force him to socialize.

On September 19 and 21, Tyler asked his roommate to leave him alone with a friend. According to Ravi's claims, he left the computer open so he could access his webcam and see what was happening in the room because he was concerned about theft. However, other witnesses claimed that he had also wanted to see if he could confirm that Tyler was gay.

That evening, Ravi and his friend, Molly Wei, turned on the webcam and they saw Clementi and his friend kissing each other. Ravi posted about this on his Twitter account, and later on, Wei also turned on the camera with four other people in the room (Ravi had left at this time). This time, they saw Tyler and his date kissing with their shirts off.

The next day, Tyler Clementi found out what had happened from Ravi's Twitter account. He sent an online request to receive a single room, because his roommate had been spying on him.

On September 21st, Ravi posted on his Twitter account that there would be another viewing party and that those who wanted could access the webcam remotely as well. He pointed the webcam at Tyler's bed and left the room. Upon his arrival, Clementi noticed the camera and unplugged it, messaging a friend about what he did. Later on, Ravi said that he was the one who had left his computer on sleep mode.

That day, Tyler complained to a resident assistant and to other officials as well and he asked if he could receive a separate room and requested that Ravi be punished for violating his intimacy in such a way. He also wrote a formal email request towards the resident assistant and quoted Ravi's Twitter messages as evidence. Also, he posted his detailed account on what had happened on Just Us Boys and on some Yahoo! message boards.

On September 22nd, Tyler went to have dinner and headed towards the George Washington Bridge. Once he got there, he posted a message on Facebook about throwing himself off the bridge and he apologized for it. Although he left a suicide note and although there were computer documents that were about to be used in the trial, they did not incriminate Ravi and his actions as the motive behind his suicide.

Ravi apologized to Tyler right after he saw his message on Facebook, trying to remove all incrimination from him. He mentioned that he was the one to remove the webcam the second night. He said that he had known Tyler to be gay as well and that he had gay friends and had nothing against people in the gay community. However, at the trial the prosecutor brought evidence to sustain that these words came after the University had already inflicted punishment on Ravi and that the entire message was nothing but a way to remove the guilt off his shoulders.

On September 28th, both Dharun Ravi and Molly Wei were charged with four and two accounts of violation of privacy, respectively. Later on, Dharun Ravi was also charged with hate crime. Although he deleted the messages he had sent Wei telling her not to say anything about the messages that he had posted on Twitter, Ravi was found guilty, together with Molly Wei.

Later on, Molly Wei's attorney reached an agreement with the prosecutors in which she would not be sentenced to jail, but she would have to do community service as well as a 3-year intervention program. Tyler's parents agreed to this because Wei had been cooperative during the investigation.

At the same time, Ravi, who was a citizen of India and a legal resident in the US, refused an agreement plea, stating that he was not guilty. He was sentenced with a 30-day imprisonment, with 300 hours of community service, 3 years of probation and a fine of $10,000 for all the 15 counts of his webcam spying activity.

Many were shocked to hear Tyler Clementi's story, and there was a wave of reactions to it. Rutgers University decided that they should give their students the right to choose their roommates regardless of their sex and that this would be done for those in the LGBTQ community to feel safer and more comfortable with their roommates. Schools in the area held a vigil for Tyler and students and staff at Tyler's high school wore black as a way to mourn his death.

President Obama, Secretary of State Hillary Clinton, and Secretary of Education Arne Duncan stood up for the rights of those bullied and expressed their deep sadness regarding the events at Rutgers. Furthermore, a federal legislation was introduced which obliged universities who wanted to receive funding from the government to establish anti-bullying procedures and codes of conduct. The law was criticized for the fact that it includes only certain groups of people and excludes others, but it can still be considered to be a huge step forward when It comes to educating people on the idea that bullying is wrong and that words, even when spoken on the Internet, still have a great power to hurt people in their real life. Furthermore, New Jersey passed a bipartisan Anti-Bullying Bill of Rights which was voted in almost unanimously.

Celebrities also stood up for Tyler Clementi's story and they expressed their sadness, grief and shock at the hearing of the news. Among them, Ellen DeGeneres openly spoke about the fact that more and more teenagers are committing suicide because of bullying and that something needs to be done in order for this to stop. Several artists also included Tyler's story in their work as a way of raising awareness over cyberbullying and LGBTQ youth issues.

Tyler's parents established a charitable foundation that aims to help troubled LGBT community teenagers and young people and which also aims to educate people against all forms of bullying, including online bullying.

The story behind the death of Tyler Clementi can be emotional and it is probably one of the most shocking cases of its kind. As a young and talented student, Tyler had a world full of possibilities ahead of him: he had opened up to his mother and father about his sexuality, he had even started dating someone and he was a student at a good college, doing something he liked. However, depression and torment overcame him and he eventually killed himself.

In the light of Tyler's story, the black hole of cyberbullying in which many teenagers and young people are attracted was seen once again. The Internet enabled Tyler's roommate to do what he did and it was the Internet that delivered the troubled young man's last message, the same way it delivered him with the humiliation, rejection and deep sadness. The Internet was a big part of Tyler's life, but it was its end as well when his most intimate actions were ruthlessly shared with other students on campus. Adding this to our world's automatic rejection of the LGBTQ community, the situation quickly escalated into tragedy.

# Phoebe Prince

The story of Phoebe Prince shook the state of Massachusetts and forced officials to acknowledge that anti-bullying laws need to be enacted before it is too late for other children. Even more, the entire world was shown once again that bullying is a serious matter in the United States and around the world.

Born in Bedford, England in 1994, Phoebe Prince was about to become another well-known victim of bullying. She and her parents moved from England to Ireland when she was only 2. In 2009, Phoebe, her siblings and her mother immigrated to the United States, in Boston, while her father stayed in Ireland.

This is when the problems started to arise for young Phoebe and it is the moment that would lead up to her suicide later on. As a new kid at the South Hadley High School, Phoebe Prince was soon bullied by some of her classmates and the taunting did not stop. In December, she had disputes with two girls.

According to the family's testimony, the school knew about these bullies, but did nothing. Phoebe's aunt claims that she had warned the school officials that Phoebe may be susceptible to things such as bullying and that they should keep an eye on her. However, it turned out that Phoebe was herself involved in a case of bullying back in Ireland and that she had been bullying a girl with another friend of hers over an issue related to a boy. After that girl was moved to a different school, Phoebe admitted her blame and asked the girl for forgiveness. Eventually, the bullied victim's parents blamed the peer pressure for Phoebe's actions and they forgave her as well.

In January, 3 of the accused teenagers in the case of Phoebe Prince persistently taunted the young girl at school, in the library and in the auditorium. One of them followed Phoebe home in a friend's car and at a certain point threw an empty can at her and insulted her. It was after this incident that Phoebe went home and committed suicide by hanging herself. She was found by her younger sister, who at the time was only 12.

A Facebook memorial page was opened for Phoebe Prince, but many people chose to post crude comments about her suicide there. These comments were erased later on.

Immediately after her death, the school held a meeting in which they discussed the officials who knew about the bullying issues that arose around the school.

Furthermore, the state of Massachusetts soon sped up anti-bullying legislation enactment and New York State followed suit. Furthermore, a "Phoebe's Law" was proposed at a national level in an attempt to try to build a stronger legislation against bullying in the United States.

In March, the D.A. Elizabeth Scheibel came out and publicly admitted that two boys and four girls were indicted with felony charges. Among these charges were violation of civil rights, criminal harassment, and stalking and even statutory rape. Furthermore, three of the four girls who had bullied Phoebe Prince were indicted with delinquency complaints and one of them was accused of assault with a deadly weapon (because she had thrown the empty can at Phoebe). Furthermore, another three of the girls involved in the bullying of Phoebe were accused with assault and battery against another student of the same high school who had appeared on TV to describe the bullying issues in her school.

Scheibel also mentioned that a large part of the student body in that school, as well as some of the teachers knew about the bullying that was going on. Adding this to the entire school's lack of understanding about harassment and/or the dating relationships that were taking place between their students, it has become clearer how the entire situation escalated to such proportions.

The District Attorney also urged schools to start their own fight against such cases by properly training their staff, as well as by organizing meetings with their students that would help them understand situations similar to this one and solve them before it is too late. Also, she urged Phoebe's parents to rely on the criminal justice system and not to try to seek for their own justice by any means.

The six teenagers charged with various forms of felony went to court, raising another question: are they young enough to be allowed to make mistakes or should they be punished severely, the same way as an adult would be in the same situation? In the end, the bullies were publicly humiliated and they were even harassed in their own turn by people who had found out where they lived. Furthermore, the accused teenagers lost important things in their lives due to this trial: some of them lost their college scholarships, others lost one year of their lives without going to school, and so on.

It appears that the South Hadley High School had other issues with bullying as well. An Asperger's student in the same high school (a former friend of Phoebe Prince) has a civil lawsuit against the school for having neglected the fact that she was bullied and for not having taken any kind of measure against those who did it.

Bullying is, as this story shows, a two-sided coin. On the one hand, everybody can turn into a victim in a society where bullying is considered a rite of passage. It is considered far too normal to have our children bullied in school and to believe that threatening, harassment, and other such crimes are actually helping kids grow up into better or stronger people. Phoebe Prince's bullies may be faulty, but in the end, they are just children themselves and pressing criminal charges against them to burden them for the rest of their lives may not be the best solution.

Many people believe that avoiding the kind of situations in which Phoebe found herself starts with better communication: between classmates and friends, between students and teachers, between children and their parents and between parents and teachers. In Phoebe's case, it appeared that nothing worked as it should and this is what led to her eventually committing suicide.

Understanding where bullying comes from and why has it gotten so far will be important for the future. Phoebe's case has not only raised awareness of how deadly bullying can be, but it has also helped people realize that, in the end, bullies are also children who are confused, scared, and who want to push aside everything that is different from them. They have self-confidence issues as well; they may come from broken families and they may have darker pasts than you would imagine. In the end, they are the result of their environment. Their understanding of bullying and what its consequences can be is frequently limited and it does not paint the entire picture. At the same time, campaigns in school are often inefficient and badly chosen for the age group of students they are presented to, which undermines their effectiveness.

# Jamey Rodemeyer

Jamey Rodemeyer's story touched the world and showed that both homophobia and bullying are real issues among the American youth. An openly gay teen, Jamey Rodemeyer encouraged and supported other people like him through his YouTube videos. Eventually, bullying and harmful words became stronger than his optimism and he gave in to the pressure.

Born in 1997, Jamey lived near Buffalo, New York. A graduate of the Heim Middle School, he was just in his freshman year at Williamsville North High School when he died. A great fan of Lady Gaga, he was inspired by her music to come out and to talk openly about his sexuality in order to help others like him.

Although he was constantly harassed even in middle school because of his sexuality (some of his online accounts revealed this clearly), Jamey had the courage to help others, which many people who are older than he is still don't find the power to do. He constantly advised people through his YouTube videos and he even made a video as part of the It Gets Better project that was created to prevent suicide among teenagers. Unfortunately, Jamey's bullies appeared stronger for the moment and on the morning of September 18, 2011, the 14-year old boy was found by his sister, hanged. The last message on his Twitter account bid farewell to his idol, Lady Gaga.

Police officials conducted an investigation for 9 weeks after Jamey's death and although they found multiple incriminating messages both on his computer and on his mobile phone, they could not prosecute anybody for Jamey's death. Most of the criminal harassment accusations were unable to be sustained by actual evidence and when this was possible, it was expired by the statute of limitations.

An earthquake of reactions came after Jamey's death. As he was popular on the Internet for his YouTube and Tumblr account, many people felt close to him and saw in him a model and an encouragement. Jamey's online supporters and real-life friends came together to mourn the loss of their friend.

At the same time, the bullies who had tormented Jamey's life at school did not appear to change their mind. When Jamey's sister attended a school dance, when a Lady Gaga song was played, some of his friends present at the dance started to chant his name. Meanwhile, the bullies started to chant that they were happy that Jamey had committed suicide.

Jamey is not the only similar case and although many people refuse to accept that bullying has to be dealt with, awareness has been raised for the past few years, especially after such terrible cases. Teenagers committed suicide as a result of the bullying they faced in school and online.

Parents of the victims spoke about their story, hoping to prevent this kind of thing happening again. Jamey's parents did this as well and they openly admitted that even after Jamey's death, the entire family was still bullied over his suicide (including Jamey's brother and sister) and that they were tormented by malicious words and even threats.

Lady Gaga admitted that she was devastated by the death of this young fan. In one of her tour concerts, she dedicated her song to Jamey, thanking him for the great example that he had set by standing out for his own identity and by trying to help others who were in the same situation.

Furthermore, she even had a meeting with President Barack Obama and they discussed how bullying in schools should be addressed. Cases such as Jamey's are, unfortunately, frequently encountered nowadays and the truth is that foundations, politicians, celebrities, spokespeople, parents and teachers can come together and change something for the thousands of children who suffer every day because of the venomous words and actions inflicted upon them by other children.

Another celebrity that started to speak out for the kids who are constantly bullied was Miss New York Kaitilin Monte, who made an online petition to support the enactment of new cyberbullying laws in New York. Soon after that, New York senator Jeffrey Klein proposed the legislation. The two of them joined their forces to create the New York Cyberbully Census.

Actor Zachary Quinto stated that Jamey's story had impressed him so much that he decided it was time for him to come out as gay as well. According to his statement, not coming out and living openly as a gay person means not making one's contribution towards equality and the great fight that is given in the name of the LGBTQ community. Up to that moment, Zachary Quinto had denied the rumors that appeared in press, but in the light of the events that followed Jamey's death, he decided that something has to be done in order to stop children such as Jamey killing themselves again because they are constantly harassed by homophobic bullying.

The TV show Glee also made a reference to Jamey Rodemeyer in an episode that touched on the issue of gay teenage suicide. Also, Dan Kloeffer openly came out as a gay man immediately after Zachary Quinto.

Celebrities and coverage in the media may not be able to bring back the tormented kids who fell victims to bullying and cyberbullying, but they are an important "weapon" in making people understand that these things are serious. The rate of suicide among teenagers and the relationship between the depression that had led them to that point and the constant bullying they had to face out are connected, and more and more people acknowledge that the matter should be treated more seriously.

In his huge-heartedness, Jamey Rodemeyer tried to make people understand that being gay should not be considered to be wrong and that there is nothing in the world that should make kids like him feel discriminated upon. Eventually, depression and bullying caught him but his story will live forever as a testimony of the fact that such issues have to be taken into consideration by everybody surrounding the kids: their parents, their friends, their teachers and, ultimately, themselves. The LGBTQ community will always be thankful for Jamey and for having made such a huge difference in many people's hearts. Same way, even children who are not bullied as a result of their place in this community should join together and stand up for their own rights. Together with teachers and parents, as well as with the huge number of celebrities ready to sustain their cause, these kids can make a difference in the world.

Jamey Rodemeyer's mother is a true example of how parents should react when their kids are bullied in school: she took action and talked to teachers and the school principal. On the other hand, the school could have reacted more promptly in defending Jamey and the entire tragedy may have been avoided.

The reaction the mother had after the death of her son is even more impressive. Having the power to stand up and fight for the rights of those in the same situation as your son and not wanting to obtain revenge of any kind shows true character, and it is something more parents should do.

It is a mad world, and children are most affected by the lack of understanding from adults and from their peers. It starts with education and with raising your children not to be bullies. It starts with making everybody know that stories such as Jamey's have become too frequent to be ignored.

# Alexis Pilkington

Sometimes, even popular students become victims of bullying. Alexis Pilkington's story is of this kind. This should, again, raise some questions for all the sides involved in these bullying cases: school officials, lawmakers and parents at the same time because, in one way or another, the entire society is to blame for the death of these young people.

Alexis Pilkington was set up to succeed in life: she was beautiful, smart, and an excellent athlete who had already received a college scholarship for her soccer talent. However, she soon became a victim of bullying and joined the large numbers of teens who committed suicide because of these malicious acts.

Her parents chose not to share a lot of details about their daughter's life. Although no evidence of her bullying has been presented (not at school, not on the Internet and not anywhere else for that matter), the police have investigated this issue particularly due to the events that followed her death.

According to her father's statements, Alexis had personal trouble she had to face and she had been under therapy for a while before she committed suicide. However, this did not help her, as in March 2010 she was found dead by suicide. The actual means of her death were never disclosed to the public and her death remains a mystery.

Her father is himself a policeman and he does not seem to take the option of bullying and cyberbullying into consideration when it comes to the reasons that pushed Alexis into suicide. However, nasty messages the 17-year-old girl received soon before her death, as well as the messages left by various anonymous people after her death, would say otherwise.

Soon after her death, people thought of opening a memorial Facebook page where they could remember Alexis. This Facebook page was soon filled with malicious comments on Alexis' personality, sexually suggestive comments, and many other bad things. Most of these things were left anonymously and have since been erased from the page.

Although these comments cannot hurt Alexis now, they can be considered bullying because they are addressed more to the mourners of Alexis' death than to Alexis. The bullies who do this may not even realize how much their words can affect those who suffer after the young girl's death and they may not see that the Facebook page was created to allow people to grieve in peace over the loss of a friend, colleague and family member.

One of Alexis' friends yelled at the sight of these comments and the girl's mother recalls the horror on her other daughter's face the moment she saw what people had been posting about Alexis online after her death.

Some of the people who were mourning Alexis and who were outraged by the Facebook comments contacted a Facebook spokesperson and told him about their issue. Soon, the spokesperson publicly stated that all the accounts that are found to be in any way related to malicious comments and cyberbullying on this page would be immediately terminated.

Malicious comments had been posted on Formspring as well, a website Alexis had signed up for not much before her death. An anonymous spokesperson also claimed that Alexis' friends had the right to mourn her in peace and that they would terminate accounts that are related to cyberbullying because they believed that Alexis' friends should not have to face such disgraceful words on their friend.

When he was contacted to make a comment on the post-death cyberbullying that had been going on, New York Police Department officer Pilkington refused to make a statement. He agreed to cooperate with the authorities, but he believed his daughter's suicide had nothing to do with the cyberbullying she faced. Although Alexis had been a troubled teenager before she was bullied, many people do not exclude the idea that the bullying made the situation worse for her and eventually contributed to her suicide.

Alexis' father believes that his daughter's suicide did not have anything to do with bullying and that the things that were affecting her previous to the bullying messages were significant to a larger extent. However, he has come out to speak about the Facebook and Formspring malicious comments and he said that the bullies should at least attach a name and a face to the horrible things they said.

Many of the psychologists and experts in this field believe that cyberbullying can have serious consequences on the life of teenagers and that its effects may be sometimes be harsher than those inflicted by real-life bullying. According to this school of thought, cyberbullying leaves victims with a feeling that they are generally disliked because the bully can hide under a cloak of anonymity, leaving the victim guessing their identity, but ultimately unable to associate a face with the malicious comments.

It is estimated that out of all the victims of cyberbullying, more than 50% never actually get to know the bully's face or real name. Many of them live on feeling that they are generally disliked and that the hurtful words are the voicing out of what everybody else believes in. Also, studies do show the fact that cyberbullying can be considered a major cause in creating a more and more troubled youth.

The main issue with cyberbullying is that although over the past few years, the world has seen countless suicide cases among bullied teens, many people refuse to accept that bullying and cyberbullying are real issues. As mentioned before, many people see being bullied as a rite of passage, and many parents and teachers close their eyes and their ears to complaints from kids who are tormented by their fellow classmates.

Acknowledging cyberbullying as an issue is definitely the first step towards finding a solution and towards implementing prevention programs. Cases such as Alexis' are not unique, and even at her school some parents decided to talk openly about the death of their own child not long before Alexis' death. According to the people's account, they do not remember Alexis being present at the meeting.

Maybe that discussion would have saved her life, and maybe it did save the life of those who were there to hear and participate in it. Maybe more discussions of this kind in all the schools would help people to understand that tormenting someone is not right and that it can have real-life consequences. As you have seen, cyberbullying can take many shapes and it can come in various ways, but in the end it affects sensitive children and it leads an alarming number of them into the hands of death.

The Internet has definitely provided people with access to information and communication like there never was before. At the click of a mouse, you can learn about anything in the world, you can watch any movie, you can buy music that will soothe your soul, and you can chat with a friend who lives on the other side of the Earth.

There are certain advantages to the Internet, but with it, new and horrible dangers for our children have appeared as well. Protecting them from the invisible, especially when they want their own privacy, can be difficult but not impossible. Protecting them from the tremendous number of cyberbullies and sex offenders online is not easy, but it is certainly doable once you set your mind to it. Sooner or later, your kids will understand why you are taking all these precautions and they will thank you for it. Learning how to use the Internet for their own benefit and not for their own destruction will have to be part of their education from now on, and so will the dangers of being a bully, for both of these matters are much more serious than a child's game.

# Carl Joseph Walker-Hoover

Carl Joseph Walker-Hoover's story is even more revealing when it comes to the importance parents and teachers play in the bullying process. Although they may not be the ones enforcing the bullying, they are still the ones who do not take measures against it in many cases (or if they do, their measures are simply inefficient).

Carl was only 11 when he committed suicide by hanging himself with a cord. Up to that moment, no one could have predicted that he would do such a terrible thing. He was involved in multiple extra-curricular activities, such as athletics and the Boy Scouts. People describe him as someone who was there to help whenever it was needed, and that he truly had the soul of a Boy Scout. People agree that he was talented and smart and that he would have succeeded in life if it weren't for the bullying he faced.

His mother was fierce when it came to protecting her children. When Carl came home the first time and told her that kids had been picking on him and calling him gay at school, Sirdeaner Walker did something about it. She took action against the bullying, talking to a number of school officials. However, this was not enough, as the malicious comments continued.

According to Sirdeaner's statements, Carl was not even facing sexuality issues before his death. Although kids suspected he was gay, and although the entire LGBTQ community supported his mother after the boy's death, the mother openly stated that she does not even believe Carl had matured enough to consider his sexuality.

Even more, she believes that bullying is an issue that goes beyond LGBTQ rights, because it is a problem that does not affect the LGBTQ community exclusively. She has expressed her worry over the fact that many kids are picked on in schools for being overweight or just different than the vast majority. This is why she believes bullying should be an area of concern for everyone.

In memory of her lost son, Sirdeaner has opened a foundation aimed at helping people see the importance of bullying prevention. Bullying is not a game among children, and the shocking number of deaths associated with teen bullying and cyberbullying should alarm everybody.

Just as she had been fierce in protecting Carl and her other three kids, Sideaner wants to be fierce now in the name of those who suffer as her own boy did. According to her statements, she wants to focus on studying bullying policy and on finding a solution to it. To her, the issue of bullying lies at the core of our society and she believes that instead of worrying about wars, people should pay more attention to how bullying has caused the death of thousands of children both in the United States and around the world.

Researchers at Yale University have managed to find a connection to stand as evidence of the ties of bullying, depression, and suicide. Even more, other studies show that although suicides are uncommon at Carl's age, their numbers are increasing at an alarming rate.

Many of the specialists believe that school officials do not act against bullying in general (and against homophobic bullying in particular) because gay rights are still a controversial issue in the United States, and they do not want to create tension with conservative parents. Carl's death is not the only one associated with homophobic comments and bullying, but it is a story that shook the world.

To some, homosexuality is considered either taboo or just a topic of discussion that is best avoided. Many people believe that the bullies themselves are victims of a society that has taught them that homosexuality is wrong and that they should banish homosexuals from their lives.

Walker is a true survivor and she knows that she will not stop until she has given her last breath to the cause of anti-bullying campaigns. According to her, she has been through homelessness and domestic violence. It is crucial that such strong men and women get involved in anti-bullying campaigns, because the world is still full of people who think bullying is normal.

As mentioned before, it all starts with teaching kids not to let words harm who they truly are on the inside. Furthermore, teachers and parents should educate themselves in order to guide kids when a bullying case arises.

Hate speech discrimination can have tragic consequences. When they are related to the future of the children in this country though, they become more serious than anything. In the end, the bullies who say these things are, in their own turn, victims of abuse or just victims of negligence from the behalf of their environment. Many bullies come from split families, from families where domestic violence is the norm and from families that are dysfunctional in one way or another.

Furthermore, bullying is associated with the main ideas that dominate our society. For example, many people who bully members of the LGBTQ community use their beliefs to justify their actions — they may believe that homosexuality is wrong and that it is their duty to change people. For Carl Walker, society played an important role, and his case is not unique.

Carl was just 11 years old when he died, but his story will be forever fresh both in the minds of those who knew him and in the minds of those who found out about him. His story is heartbreaking and maddening, but his mother hopes that both Carl's story and the stories of many other kids in similar situations will be a wakeup call for the education system, for lawmakers, for parents, and for the society that pushes these kids to suicide.

Children committing suicide is something everybody should consider horrendous, and it should be a huge cause for alarm for everyone. As a symbol of youth and purity, children have to be protected and they have to be made to understand that they are important for the world.

Shocking as it may seem, many people are still not aware of these things happening. When these stories come into the news, people nod their heads in disapproval and blame everyone but themselves for allowing these things to happen. But in the end, we are all responsible, because we are all part of a society that pushes away what is different and that wants to teach children how to become grownups "the hard way." This is not always the best way and the death of an 11-year-old should make everybody understand this.

Understanding, peace, and support — this is what kids need for a better future. They need to know that they are here with a purpose and that adults are there to support them in times of trouble. They need to know that their teachers will protect them and that their peers will understand them.

# Lee Simpson

The issue of bullying is definitely not limited just to the United States. Stories such as those presented here have happened in other parts of the world as well. Lee Simpson's death stands as evidence for the fact that both social acceptance of the LGBTQ community and bullying are important international issues that have to be addressed as soon as possible, before the number of teen suicides rises to an even more alarming level.

About one year before his death, 18-year-old Lee Simpson wrote a letter in which he openly admitted that he was gay. His father accepted him and all of his close friends had no issue with it. Society, on the other hand, started to point out fingers at Lee for coming out.

Soon after coming out, Lee started receiving anonymous calls harassing him for his sexuality. As his father now recounts, he picked up most of these calls and never actually told Lee about them. However, Lee did pick up some of them, and he was terribly upset by the anonymous harassment.

Born in Manchester, Lee was about to become yet another symbol of the struggles the young members of the LGBTQ community experience. As his father has told newspapers, Lee had never been traditionally masculine, and he was taking special treatment for this. But Lee's coming out as gay did not stop his father from loving him unconditionally and from accepting him just the way he was.

Lee's story can very well portray the complexity of being gay in our world and when taking a closer look at the reasons that pushed this young and promising boy into committing suicide, one realizes that things go far beyond bullying. They are deeply rooted in the subconscious of society, including in those who are the victims of bullying.

The harassing phone calls Lee received were a part of the story that would become significant in understanding why Lee had killed himself. In a way, these phone calls were the voice of an entire society that points fingers at those who are different. For some people, being a homosexual is something unimaginable, sinful, and wrong. While most of the people would choose not to say anything about this, Lee's bullies chose to constantly harass him to the point where he could not take it anymore. The childcare student was found hanged in his home months after the series of calls actually begun.

As mentioned, Lee Simpson's father recalls that he openly admitted that his son was gay and that he had no issues with it. He does remember, however, that the one who struggled with this newly acknowledged identity was Lee himself. According to his father, Lee had always been religious, and he now believes that this may have influenced the boy's descent into depression and eventual suicide.

Lee's opinion of himself was the opinion of a society that thinks that being gay is a sin, that it is unnatural, and that it is something to be ashamed of. The teenage years are often filled with trouble and torment, especially when it comes to finding one's identity. For people in the LGBTQ community, things are made even more difficult because society will shoot nasty words at them whenever it gets the chance. For the LGBTQ community, finding their own identity is a continuous struggle.

If you add these factors to the bullying Lee faced, one can understand how the situation escalated to a point where Lee could not take it any longer. Self-esteem issues are common among all teenagers, but those who stand out will be automatically be tagged as "different" and put to the wall of infamy.

Lee was different, but not in a bad way. He was troubled, he had self-confidence issues, and he had trouble accepting his own identity. Constant harassment, his issues with himself, and a society and religion that labels gays as sinful — these were the three main factors that contributed to Lee's death.

Despite our differences, we are all human. Understanding this is essential when it comes to preventing situations such as Lee's. People often fear everything that is different, and fearful people can become angry, mean, and frustrated. If more people spoke openly about how it is to be part of the LGBTQ and if people would be more open to understanding this, cases such as Lee's would be much less common.

Lee's problem was one of acceptance. His father's statement stands as proof that Lee had problems truly accepting who he was. The bullies had issues understanding both who Lee was and that their harmful words could lead to this. Acceptance would have been a solution for Lee, and it still is a solution for the thousands and thousands of kids who find themselves in the same situation.

Lee's story took place in the United Kingdom, which shows that bullying and homophobia are international issues that should be addressed as quickly as possible. The media coverage shows how so many teenagers committed suicide over the past few years as a result of bullying. These numbers will not decrease unless people decide to make a change.

Laws to protect kids from harassment have to be enacted, but the world also needs strong campaigns to make people understand and accept that "different" does not mean "bad" and that bullying must be taken seriously. The deaths of so many children stand as evidence that change has to occur not only in legislation and in the ways schools treat the problem of bullying, but in our minds as well.

It may be years before the LGBTQ community is safe from harassment. It may be another generation before things like this will completely disappear. Since many young people already accept "being different" as part of the natural course of humanity, which shows that hope is not lost and that if action is taken today, our tomorrow may be much better and much more peaceful.

Speaking out and encouraging kids to stand up for who they are will help, but the most important thing is to make them feel important, safe, supported, and understood. These things usually lie at the foundation of treating depression. Lee Simpson's story is just one of many, and sensitizing public opinion will help. These boys and girls should not die in vain, and they should set a true example for the people still believing that bullying is okay.

# Eric Mohat

Eric Mohat was yet another victim of bullying and the flawed way schools deal with this issue. A student at Mentor High School, Eric was thin, tall, outstandingly smart, and talented at music. He was the perfect sensitive target for bullies, who told him the world would be much better off without him in it.

From being hit and pushed to being called names, Eric Mohat endured terrible bullying. Yet, Mentor High School apparently did nothing, which is why Eric's parents have decided to sue the school. They did not ask for monetary compensation. Instead, they asked that the school acknowledge guilt and establish an efficient bullying prevention program. The lawsuit stated that Eric had been called various names in the presence of his teachers. As adults, they had the moral obligation to stand up for the boy — yet, they didn't and the situation quickly escalated to the death of a talented and warm-hearted boy.

Unfortunately, it seems this kind of behavior among teachers and school officials has become the norm in Mentor High School. School officials confirmed that three other students committed suicide the same year. Even though the school did not admit these suicides were related to bullying, there was evidence to suggest it. One of Eric's friends was even moved to a different school by his parents because he faced constant bullying from his classmates, and the teachers failed to intervene. Officials at Mentor High School have tried to hide this from the public to protect the school's reputation, but soon enough the truth surfaced.

The torment Eric faced was mostly of a verbal and usually related to him supposedly being gay. The fact that he was into drama and the fact that he wore bright clothes made his classmates make fun of him and label him as gay, although there had been no evidence of this fact. Furthermore, they frequently threw things in his hoodies and bothered him by flicking him in the ear. Although Mohat told his teacher about this, the only thing the school official did was to move the bullies' desks.

On March 27, 2007, the bullies went much farther than accusing Eric of being gay. They told him the thing that would push him to commit suicide: that the world would be better off without him. Eric Mohat went home to his father's bureau drawer, pulled out his father's gun, and shot himself in the head. The first one to discover him was his sister, Erin, with whom Eric had been very close.

Eric's parents decided to file a lawsuit. The school continued to deny the accusations, claiming that they had no idea of what was going on and that they had no involvement in the events. When the lawsuit was filed, the school communications manager openly admitted that the school deserved blame.

Mentor High School has a true issue with bullying. They are already using an anti-bullying program. However, this program is addressed to kindergarten and primary school students and that it is completely unsuitable for teenagers. Even more, the basic idea behind this anti-bullying program was that bullies feel bad about themselves and picking on others makes them feel good. While this may be true in some cases, situations can vary and potential victims of bullying should be informed.

When Eric told his parents about the bullying, he also told them that the teacher had handled it and it would not happen again. However, just a few days before he killed himself, he told his mother that he could not handle it any longer because there were many school weeks left in the year.

Eric's mother and his father are now advocating for those in the same situation as their son. They are not asking for anything other than attention to be given to these children and to bullying in general. As Eric's father puts it, schools tend to give a lot of attention to things that are much less significant than the children being tormented by their peers every day. Sports, events, and administrative things come first, while anti-bullying programs are tacked on as an afterthought.

When bullying occurs on school grounds, school officials become witnesses. Many people still have a mentality based on the idea that bullying is part of growing up and that it is something that goes away on its own. For Eric and many other children, growing up was hard enough even without bullying and when torments began, they took these kids' desire to live.

Statistics show terrifying numbers when it comes to bullying. According to the National Youth Violence Prevention Center, no less than 30% of the kids in school are being bullied during their education. This makes for nearly one-third of the total students, which is an especially alarming number when taking into consideration the tragic effects of bullying.

Another set of research shows that almost 160,000 children in the United States choose to stay home every day because they are scared that they will go to school and be bullied and picked on.

Yale also conducted research in this field and the findings are terrifying indeed. According to their statistics after studying 13 countries, five of them had serious issues related to bullying. In these countries, bullied children were two to nine times more likely to commit suicide, due to the relationship between teen suicide and bullying.

Numbers are nothing, though, when compared to these tragic and horrendous stories. Most people have heard about at least one of these teen suicide cases, and many who hear this remain shocked at the idea that somewhere, this entire system is wrongly built. It seems that nobody cares until somebody dies and that even when children kill themselves, people do not seem to care enough to take action.

Yet, action can and should be taken immediately, because anyone's children can end up in the same situation. Even bullies themselves can become victims. Children in high school and in middle school are vulnerable and confused, which can turn them into bullies or victims.

Many celebrities and public figures have become aware of the issue. In the last few years, more and more laws have been enacted to protect children from bullying. Although there are still many instances of suicide, the world is on a better path than it was 10 years ago. Action will be taken and the terror in schools will lessen. Communication, laws, and building better anti-bullying campaigns are the solution to this huge problem the world is faced with.

# Brandon Myers

Suicide is always an awful thing, but when it robs you of your child, things can become unbearable. Brandon Myers was only 12 when he committed suicide, and for him, life had never been easy.

Born with a cleft palate, Brandon fought long and hard under the knife to get where he was. Although he still had a visible speech impairment issue, he was strong and he went to school just like the other kids. His parents divorced when he was five, which added to his already sensitive condition. When he was in the third grade, doctors diagnosed him with attention deficit hyperactivity disorder and later on, he was diagnosed with depression. These conditions forced Brandon to take medication every day.

Other than that, Brandon was like any other kid his age. As his parents recall, he loved fishing and he would even wake up early in the morning to fish in the nearby pond with a friend, Trystyn Wagner. Now, Trystyn misses his friend terribly and his mother is afraid that the sadness will overwhelm him as well. She knows that the two friends had fought over a girl a few days prior Brandon's death, but that they made up as well. For Trystyn, though, guilt is a heavy burden – much too heavy for a 12-year-old who had just lost his best friend. Trystyn's mother decided that he would have to move schools because of the bullies he faced there.

That is how Brandon's story went. There are multiple accounts of him being bullied in school. Teachers and other school officials failed to stop these bullies, despite clear signs that this was happening right under their noses.

For example, Trystyn found a picture Brandon drew of himself hanging, and turned it in to the teacher, but nothing happened. Later evidence has also showed that Brandon told some of his friends that he was going to commit suicide by hanging. Brandon wrote another friend a note, telling him he would kill himself before 4:35, and that he should alert two of his other friends. The note was later found by the boy's mother and turned in to the police, but the Myers did not find out about it until 3 months later.

Brandon's struggles had been pointed out to the teachers as well, but no measure has been taken to support the boy. In December 2007, he wrote in a school assignment that he was sorry for being the one to stand outside the circle, for being different than the other children in his class. This shows that Brandon had been fighting depression and acceptance issues for quite a while before he hung himself.

Brandon Myers' parents did not want to leave things like this. In the wake of the many teen and child suicides, they know that taking action is important. This is why they are suing the Blue Springs School District for their son's death. According to them, signs of trouble had been there for a long time, but the Voy Spears Elementary School staff failed to stop the bullying that eventually led to Brandon's death. Even more, teachers did not notify Brandon's mother, and she learned of all these signs only when it was already much too late.

The case is not without precedent; there was another case of a boy who was bullied for allegedly being gay. His family later sued the school district and settled for $440,000 for harassment charges when the boy was close to graduating school. The bullying had started when he was in the 7th grade.

There are many other accounts of parents trying to get justice for their kids and trying to advocate for stronger anti-bullying policies in school. Although Blue Springs had a policy against bullying and although it included electronic forms of bullying, the officials failed to notify Brandon's parents on the struggles their boy had to face.

The circumstances in which Brandon was tormented by his classmates and the kind of bullying he faced are not yet disclosed to the public, as the parents and their attorney believe that this would sacrifice the integrity of their trial.

Brandon is not a singular case. It is estimated that between 1999 and 2004, more than 1,600 teenagers committed suicide. Although adolescents tend to be more susceptible to this, the number of younger children doing it has increased dramatically.

In Missouri alone, no less than 34 cases of suicide among children and teens were taken into account and Megan Meier's case is just one of many. At a national level, it is believed that 30% of the students in the American schools have faced bullying. The vast majority of them consist of those who are bullies themselves (13%), followed closely by those who become victims of bullying (11%) and by those who are both victims and bullies themselves (6%).

This shows, once again, that bullying is a genuine problem and not just in the United States. Bullying can lead to suicide and as it has been pointed out, there seems to be a close connection between bullying and teen suicide. The numbers are even more alarming when related to the total number of children in educational institutions and when you consider that for every bullied kid, there is a high chance of suicide.

The most worrisome issue at hand is that Brandon's school has chosen not to take any kind of action. Like in many cases already presented, adults choose not to consider that children are susceptible to bullying and that it can truly affect their feelings. For Brandon, who was already a troubled kid with health issues coming from a broken family, these bullies were like a death sentence.

Adults should be more aware of the effects bullying can have on teenagers and children, and they should take precautions to avoid these situations. The numbers of children who commit suicide is truly tragic and it is teachers' and parents' responsibility to punish those who bully their classmates. It is their duty to educate children in a way that is not hateful towards the other peers, but loving. This issue is rooted at the core of our society, a society in which the Alpha males (and females, for that matter) are celebrated.

Seeing children get bullied every day and closing your eyes to it means that, in one way or another, you take part in the bullying itself. Even if adults do not directly encourage these actions, by not punishing bullies, they are giving their silent approval.

Emphasis has to be put on building campaigns that will change kids' minds about bullying. Any moment, your own kid can become the victim of a bully, even if he/she was a bully in his/her own turn. Any moment, another child can commit suicide because of the lack of care people have for these kids. And, in the end, this falls on the shoulders of everybody who surrounded the kid.

# Karen Klein

Sometimes, the victims of bullying are not even children or people of the same age as the bullies. Karen Klein can be an inspiring story on how people can stand up for each other in times of need and for those they respect.

Karen Klein had worked on a school bus for more than 23 years at the time when the infamous "Bus monitor bullying" video came out on the Internet. For 20 years, she was a bus driver, and for the next three years, she was a monitor on the same bus. At the time the video was shot and the scandal came out, she was 68 and had eight grandchildren of her own.

Karen Klein frequently suffered from bullying from some of the kids that were riding the bus every day. However, she never pressed charges and she never said anything. When the infamous video came out though, both the Internet and the authorities were full of indignation. How could a senior member of the society go through such tremendous harassment?

In total, there were three videos posted on Facebook first, and then on a YouTube account. All of the videos showed how three boys tormented her with nasty comments. Helm, Teng, and Slesak, students in the 7th grade, were the main characters in the video. There was a fourth boy as well, Recio, who had been recording everything and who later on claimed that he did this by giving in to peer pressure.

Comments about Karen Klein's age, weight, and purse were made first. They escalated to a point where she started to cry. When they saw the woman's tears, the boys started to say it was sweat and made comments about her weight. Later, they started to poke and touch her, asking her to say her address on the video. On some occasions, the woman tried to tell them that she knew their addresses and suggested that she would tell their parents what they were doing, but the kids did not take her seriously.

One of the malicious comments made was that all the members of Klein's family had killed themselves because they could not stand her. The truth was that Karen Klein did have a son who committed suicide 10 years earlier, and this remark was the most difficult for her to bear.

Later on, Karen Klein revealed that this was not the first time she had been tormented by kids on the bus and that on one occasion she even had her hearing aids knocked out. Also, she knew that out of the four boys, two of them were the meanest, while the other two just followed along.

When the Karen Klein bullying video was posted on YouTube, it rapidly gained popularity, and millions of people watched it. Naturally, reactions came soon after, and many people chose to stand up for Karen and to help her with what she had been going through.

Among the harshest reactions were those in which the bullies themselves were bullied with life threats. The identity of the four kids was disclosed soon after the video became popular, so these threats even reached their homes. In response, Karen chose not to press charges against the boys, because she thought that it would aggravate the threats they had been receiving. Karen did, however, ask for an official apology from the boys, but when she received it, she refused it because it was insufficient.

In June 2009, the Greece Central School District suspended the boys for one academic year, and they were also required to work 50 community service hours each for the senior members of the society. They were also asked to complete a formal anti-bullying program.

When CNN anchor Anderson Cooper heard Klein's story, he also tried to do something for her. He announced on his show that the Southwest Airlines would offer to pay Karen and 9 people of her choice with tickets to Disneyland for three nights. Karen was overwhelmed with gratitude.

Among those who wanted to support Klein's cause was Max Sidorov, a nutritionist living in Toronto who claimed that he was a victim of bullying himself. In order to help the bus monitor, he started a fundraising campaign on the website Indiegogo. His goal was of $5,000, but in a few days, the money raised exceeded $500,000. By the time Klein received the money, more than $700,000 had been raised. She decided that she would donate $100,000 to create the Karen Klein Anti-Bullying Foundation, which would be part of the GiveBack Foundation.

Karen's story shows how people can come together to help a fellow human in need and distress. After dedicating almost half of her life to the bus rides for school, Karen received harassment instead of appreciation. In her case, these words went far beyond bad manners, which Karen would have surely forgiven much easier. The kids who tormented Karen not only mocked and humiliated her, but they also recorded the scene, violating Karen's privacy and the right to say "no" to such a thing. Furthermore, they made it public, not knowing that this would be the exact action that would bring them one year of suspension from school, hate mail, and threats.

It is a good sign that people reacted strongly as soon as the YouTube video went viral. Although many of them were not aware that bullying could become a huge problem for the victim (and, ultimately, for the aggressors as well), people joined together at the sight of the humiliation Karen had to go through.

Even more, the scandal surrounding Karen and the video has raised awareness of another fact: no one, not even adults, is immune to bullying. Fighting bullying is not just about protecting the victims and the potential victims, but also about trying to understand what makes people do such things. This way, bullying can be fought efficiently and removed from our lives step by step.

Maybe many of you would not have expected an old lady to be the victim of bullying, or that her aggressors be children who could have also been susceptible to bullying. But Karen Klein's story may help you understand better the proportions of this problem and how communication and properly educating children into peace, love, and respect will eventually eradicate this problem.

Bullies become victims of bullying more frequently than one might think, so it should be taken into consideration when analyzing this story. Death threats and bullying solved nothing for Karen, who was actually worried about the children and the threats they received as a result of posting the video on the Internet. In the end, communication, a punishment severe enough as to teach them a lesson, and the love of all the people is what helped Karen.

Love helped more than one victim in this case. Karen donated money towards funding other anti-bullying campaigns. People helped her and she helped them. This is how our society should be built and this is how we should raise our children. If more people acted like Karen and those who donated to her cause, this world would grow into a much more beautiful, more peaceful, and safer place for kids.

# Jade Stringer

Jade Stringer's story falls out of the ordinary because as a pretty, popular, smart girl, she did not fit the stereotype of a bullying victim. She was a perfectly healthy, beautiful girl. Jade's story can show people how many forms bullying can take and what a huge issue it is in American schools, as well as in schools all over the world.

As you have already seen, bullying does not take into consideration age, gender, medical background, sensitivity, or popularity. Bullying can appear out of nowhere, and without properly understanding the psychological mechanisms behind it, it is impossible to find a solution.

Jade Stringer was only 14 when she decided to take her own life. On the surface, it seemed she had no reason to feel so hopeless. But friends said that Jade suffered deeply. She was a beautiful young girl and that attracted the jealousy of many of her peers.

Initially, neither Jade's parents nor the authorities suspected that she was the victim of bullying, since she did not even fit into the "usual" categories of people who are bullied. But Jade's friends revealed that many of her peers had grown jealous of her popularity, which started the bullying. Furthermore, on her Facebook memorial page, many of her friends commented that she was a victim of bullying, that she did not deserve it, and that bullying was one of the main reasons behind her suicide.

Also, Jade may have been saddened by a fight with her father, during which he took her mobile phone because he believed she was using it too much. This can be related to her suicide if you take into consideration the attachment many teens have to their smartphones, and that they are a means of communicating with friends.

On June 10, 2010, Jade Stringer was rushed to the hospital after her father found that she had hanged herself. After being kept alive with life support for six days, she died.

Jade Stringer's story has raised awareness that bullying can be dangerous and that it can harshly affect someone's life. It has also showed people that anyone can be bullied. Jade was, as mentioned before, a popular girl and she was bullied because of that. This sheds a new light upon understanding bullying and how it works.

The whole world needs anti-bullying campaigns. The United States is one of the countries constantly facing such issues, but the United Kingdom is among the top ones as well. There is an acute need of people who understand the phenomena and who can create anti-bullying programs to show children and adults that bullying is a serious issue that can lead to grave consequences, such as the thousands of teen suicides that have occurred over the past decade in the United States and the United Kingdom.

Gaining a better understanding of what bullying is and how different people react to different types of bullying should be among the first steps taken to fight bullying in schools. Jade could fit the stereotypical description of a bully, and not that of the victim. But in her case, things did not fall within the stereotype, and this is why nobody would have suspected the cause of her suicide without her friends mentioning the bullying she faced.

Jade's story came as a shock — not just for those who knew her, but also for others who learned of her death. People do not expect popular people to be depressed or to become victims of bullying in any way. In fact, society naturally expects good-looking people to be successful at everything they do.

Schools need to focus less on competitiveness and more on helping each other. This will help students focus less on hate and discrimination and more on acceptance. In the end, the typical competitive attitude of high school students turned Jade into a bullying victim and eventually caused her death.

People need to acknowledge that the Internet and mobile technology can be both extremely beneficial and extremely harmful, especially for children. On the one hand, the Internet provided Jade's friends with a place where they could express their grief related to the passing of their dear one. Furthermore, if it weren't for that memorial page her friends opened for her, Jade's death would have been covered in mystery and her parents and the authorities may not have had evidence of that she was being bullied prior to her death. On the other hand, the Internet and mobile technology may have been among the causes that led Jade to commit suicide.

It is important to treat the Internet in a balanced way and to educate our children. This way, people can teach their children to reap the benefits of using such a great tool as the Internet (access to information, keeping in touch with friends and family, and so on), but they can also teach them about the dangers that may arise from using the Internet wrongly (such as for bullying or for talking with strangers) and from using the Internet too much.

Balance is key in many of the bullying-related situations. It is also important for parents to know how to teach their children to protect themselves from these things and to talk about them as soon as they arise. Bullying is an international issue and although awareness is increasing, many of the people still disregard the idea that bullying can be actually life threatening.

# Jessica Logan

Jessica Logan's story shows how quickly things can go wrong when multiple bullying-related factors are involved. Jessica was 18 when her mother found her in her bedroom, hanged, with her mobile phone on the floor. For Jessica's mother, the reasons behind the suicide of her daughter were almost impossible to understand, because she had not known what Jessica was going through until it was too late.

Her school knew, and as with other cases presented here, they did nothing to stop the bullying from happening. They did talk to one of the girls that had started the bullying, but in the end this led to nothing and Jessica continued to be tormented, both in school and online.

This entire story started when Jessica "sexted" her boyfriend nude pictures. Immediately after breaking up with her, he forwarded these pictures to four other girls. Soon enough, almost everyone at school was familiar with the pictures.

Jessica endured verbal harassment and was called a slut. The humiliation of having her naked pictures spread across the Sycamore High School, and the betrayal of her ex-boyfriend, was unbearable for her. Constant bullying and malevolence were aimed at her, even when she did nothing, and at some point, she could not take it anymore.

Jessica's mother Cynthia found out about her daughter's distress only when she started receiving notes from school saying that Jessica had been skipping classes, which she did to avoid bullies. Parts of the puzzle started to shape up in Cynthia's mind, but Cynthia did not understand the severity of the situation, even when Jessica hinted that the problems involved pictures and being called names.

After hearing about her daughter's distress, Cynthia told her she would go and talk to the parents of the girls who were bullying her. However, Jessica refused this idea, fearing that it would make her even more susceptible to bullying from those girls. However, she did acknowledge that something had to be done, not just for her own good, but for those who may suffer as a consequence of sending sexually oriented messages over the electronic media. Therefore, she decided to go on TV and to talk openly about her problem. Unfortunately, this did not help her much, as two months later she was found dead. After finding her daughter dead, Cynthia had a nervous breakdown and had to be hospitalized.

After learning what caused Jessica to want to take her life, Cynthia decided she wanted justice. She filed a lawsuit against the Sycamore High School, claiming they did not do anything to stop the bullying and that she needed money in order to cover for the hospitalization she went through as a result of her daughter's suicide.

In one way or another, the school officials were just as responsible for Jessica's suicide as those who had spread the photos were. The only thing the officials in the school did was call a student and ask her to delete the pictures and to stop talking to Jessica, which was obviously not enough. The entire school had bullied Jessica by constantly sharing the same pictures of her naked.

After suing the school, Cynthia reached a settlement with the officials and received $220,000. Although she stated she was satisfied with the settlement, she is still grieving.

Criminal charges could not be made, according to the six lawyers Cynthia visited after the death of her daughter. However, she soon discovered Aftab, an Internet website meant to inform people on the dangers the Internet can expose them to. Cynthia discovered there were criminal charges that could be pressed against those disseminating the pictures.

Aftab asked Cynthia to join them in their effort to launch a large campaign that would inform schools and children of how to protect themselves from the dangers that lurk behind the screen of a computer or a mobile phone. Cynthia agreed to help them and to openly talk about her daughter's story, in the hope that this would help other kids.

Jessica's death has brought bullying and cyberbullying to the attention of not only the school officials and press, but also to that of lawmakers in Cincinnati. Following her suicide, the state approved the so-called "Jessica Logan Act" which prevents electronic bullying and trains teachers to fight the bullying they may encounter in the schools. This act has been in effect since November 2012.

Of course, for Jessica's parents, nothing can bring back their daughter, but for many of the parents who also have children who are victims of bullying, the act can make a difference. Properly training teachers into fighting various forms of bullying is one of the most important things to do in order to reduce and hopefully eliminate bullying and harassment in schools.

Teenagers can be confused, angry, and sad without being bullied, and being harassed both when they are in school and when they are online at home can be truly exhausting. Too many have failed to stand up for who they are, which has led to a situation where bullies seem to be the kings of the world and where bullying consists of not just jokes and teasing, but of acts that destroy lives.

It is estimated that nearly half of the teenagers who own a smart phone will share pictures of themselves in various sexually charged instances. Out of all the people who receive these pictures, it is believed that nearly 15% of them will disseminate the pictures to other people. This shows why "sexting" has become almost as dangerous as Internet sex offenders when it comes to the dangers of the Internet.

Jessica's story should set an example of how horrible things can be when people do not respect their own privacy and the other people's privacy. The death of Jessica Logan does not fall on the shoulders of just a few people. The entire society is to blame, because it views bullying as part of growing up. The blame also falls on the school that did not take proper measures to prevent further bullying from happening again.

The blame also falls on the lack of information available when it comes to the dangers of Internet. Many people view the Internet as a safe place where people cannot reach you unless they know your address. However, their words can, and people should understand that words can be more powerful than anything, especially when it comes to teenagers.

The Internet can be even more dangerous than real life, because people can have a sense of anonymity and they can "run" from the place where they did something wrong. Sometimes your kid's classmates can turn into the largest danger when it comes to the Internet because their deeds and their actions can affect your child in real life as well.

# John Rosi

This story is perhaps the most shocking. Even if you have already acknowledged that educational systems do have a role to play in these bullying stories, you may think their involvement is related only to their hesitance to take action in these situations.

As shown before, many of the schools do not have anti-bullying programs that fit the age of their students. Other schools have these programs, but they may also have staff members who prefer to sweep things under the rug. In other cases, schools openly admit to the fact that they do not believe bullying to be an issue within their institution.

John Rosi's story is shocking at an entirely new level, and it raises more important questions about the effect this has on the children. John Rosi is a teacher. He was not the one to be bullied — instead, he was the one to engage in bullying a kid with other kids at Gig Harbor Middle School, where he taught a half-class on reading preparation and math for eighth graders.

Video footage showing John Rosi and the other kids in the class tormenting a young boy surfaced months after the incident occurred and created a scandal. Seeing a teacher not only fail to intervene while the children were bullying another boy under his nose, but also engage in the activities, is hard to understand for many of the parents who watched the video.

After allowing more than a dozen boys to bully Kinney, a 13-year-old student, Rosi joined them. According to his statements, he did not see this as something harmful, but as mere playing around.

However, the video does not show mere horseplay among the boys. It shows multiple students carrying a boy by his arms and legs, swinging him around, burying him under chairs, and then shoving his own socks into his mouth. In the last moments, the video shows teacher John Rosi approaching the boy and threatening to sit on him after saying nasty words to him.

John Rosi was suspended for 10 days without pay, and he now has a different job. School officials now consider the case to be closed and they believe they have punished John Rosi appropriately. According to the acting Superintendent Chuck Cuzzetto, this seemed severe enough, but the boy's parents disagreed.

The boy's mother, Karla Kinney, stated that she burst into tears when she saw how her own child was tormented in such a way in school. The actions Rosi took part in caused humiliation and easily qualify as harassment.

The boy's father, Randall Kinney, openly stated that at some point he feared for the life of his son because his son told him he wanted to commit suicide and die. Considering the fact that this was not the only bullying incident in which Kinney was the victim, his father feared that the boy would go through with it.

In a letter addressed to the district investigators, Rosi apologized for his actions, but again stated that he did not see his actions as wrong or harmful for the little boy. He also implied that these things should be considered to be normal behavior for boys.

Following these events, Kinney's son became even more upset because the other boys at school kept blaming him for Rosi's suspension. Rosi was a popular teacher and his loss disturbed some of the students there, who believed Kinney should not have spoken out about his mistreatment.

This story does not end in suicide, although the boy did have suicidal thoughts. However, it should still be alarming that society does not see bullying as anything more than child's play. It is unacceptable that Rosi allowed a student to be tormented right before his eyes, and it is unthinkable that he joined in as well. Since the adults who are supposed to protect students from bullying agree with this idea of an alpha male ruling the school, people have good reason to be worried. It is a sign of a flawed society.

In the end, the change must occur within us and within the education we provide our children. This will be the most important step towards tossing bullying away and entering an age where our children will not be afraid to go to school.

By educating our children to hate less and to love more, as well as teaching them the difference between a game or a joke and bullying, we can truly change things in time. These kinds of stories are not meant to scare you, but to make you want to take action against bullying and against those who not only accept it, but also practice it instead of protecting children.

Rosi's actions in the video should not be brushed off as a simple mistake or as a one-time incident. The kids appear to be used to doing such things in his class. His popularity among these bully students should raise a question not only among parents and children, but also among those who are supposed to inflict punishment in these cases.

Reactions to Rosi's video varied, but in the end, most agreed upon a single fact: this is unacceptable when it comes from the children, not to mention when it comes from their teacher who is supposed to be the one helping them grow into better people. While in Megan Meier's case, the mother who started the fake MySpace account may not have realized how much harm she is doing, the pain and torment was clearly visible for John Rosi and he encouraged other kids to continue.

The idea of adults tormenting children should not be acceptable in our society. Parents and teachers have the duty of hoping that in the next generation, kids will not be afraid in places where they are supposed to be safe.

All the cases presented here show how bullying defeated people in one way or another. Except for Karen's story, most of these stories are tragic. They should be an example of how things can go terribly wrong when it comes to bullying and how deeply children and teenagers can be affected.

# Whitney Kropp

While most of the stories shown in the mass media in relationship to bullying are sad and downright tragic, Whitney Kropp's story is an example of how bullying should be treated and how some people are ready to lend a hand in these situations.

Whitney Kropp's story brings hope, and although it is an exception to the rule, it does set an example on what should be done about bullying and how to remove it from our lives and the lives of our children.

As a sophomore in high school, Whitney Kropp was elected to the homecoming court. At first, she was excited to find this out, but soon her feelings turned into something different. She was humiliated to discover that some popular students in school had elected her as a prank.

Her answer to the bullies was amazing. Instead of running away and hiding, she chose to stand up to her bullies and to speak for the people who may find themselves in a similar situation.

She chose to attend the dance and when people heard about her story, they helped her get a dress and get her hair done. They did everything they could to help her feel beautiful at the dance so that she would be able to stand up to her bullies with a smile on her face.

Whitney was supported by more than 1,000 people. Her "battle" against bullying was officially won, but she is now prone to making people understand that making bullies feel like they have won is the worst thing you can do when you are a victim.

After finding out that her election to Homecoming court was a prank, Whitney asked for people's help, not knowing how many local businesses would offer to help her stand up to her bullies. Her Facebook page gathered 100,000 likes. With all this support on her back, Whitney felt like a true winner, and she used this to show other people that while bullying is harmful, it can be defeated if you are a courageous person and if you have the help of some good friends.

Whitney's story resonated throughout the entire world and people rallied to help her, even if just with a like on her page. They managed to lift up her morale by offering her their support with a full makeover and even a tiara that had been sent from an admirer who lived in Beijing. Looking at this story teaches everybody one thing: everything is possible, even defeating bullying, but you need to put a lot of heart into it and you need to believe in your cause.

Not everybody manages to be as lucky as Whitney, but it is all in the hands of those who surround bullied teenagers and children: their parents, their teachers, their friends and, ultimately, authorities that should show people bullying is a serious offense and that it should never be treated as a child's play.

The first step towards "curing" the world of bullying is to support them. Whitney received the self-confidence she deserves from her admirers and she arrived at Homecoming proudly knowing that she had won against the bullies. Furthermore, the homecoming king was a boy with Down Syndrome, which means that many people in the area acknowledged that change occurs from within.

These events should help children all over the world relieve themselves from the chains of bullying. Pop culture accepts and even encourages bullying, but stories of grief, tragedy and fighting for your own identity tell us that the world has to change when it comes to this. Many children have died and many others are hurting. It is everybody's duty to protect these teenagers and children from the harsh effects bullying can have on them.

Schools may prefer to ignore these "incidents", but they need to realize that bullying is now becoming associated with criminal behavior. Bullying can imply harassment, assault, and violation of one's privacy, and it should be punishable by law. However, this should be done carefully, as kids who bully can become victims themselves. Bullies can be like this due to their environment, and they may not even know how much harm they cause when their jokes and their pokes go too far. Imprisoning these children is not an option, but examples should be set in the schools where bullying is an issue.

There is another area we must explore: Where does this rage come from? Why do these children choose to torment other children so badly? What is it that pushes them to do this and what is it that makes society accept these actions as "normal?"

One answer comes from psychologists who believe bullies are also victims at home or that they have not been educated in respecting their peers, but in hating them for being different (such as in those cases where the victim is part of the LGBTQ community). Other people believe the answer lies in the human nature and in the "survival of the fittest" mentality.

In the end, the answer may lie in all the possibilities above and more, and the solution to the huge problem bullying has become lies in understanding, acceptance, and teaching people that being different is not the same as being bad.

Furthermore, leaving bullying behind is also dependent on the kind of support victims can seek in their families and in their teachers. The authority of a parent who advises you what to do, the support of a teacher who sees that bullying is happening and takes action against it — these things are frequently forgotten because people believe it would only make the situation worse for the victim. However, if you take into consideration the stories presented and the parents' lack of awareness, then you will discover that communication should be at the basis of "curing" schools from the plague bullying has become.

Whitney Kropp showed that bullies should not be just ignored. Her story has inspired many others because its ending is not like what the mass-media is used to — the victim won over her bullies this time. Whitney walked with her smile on her face and told everybody that no matter who bullies are or why they torment you, you should not let their actions affect you.